MODERNISM IN TS ELIOT`S THE WASTE LAND

MODERNISM IN TS ELIOT`S THE WASTE LAND

Decoding Elements of Modernism in Literature

SHAFQAT MUSHTAQ

Copyright © 2019 by SHAFQAT MUSHTAQ

[All rights reserved, including the right to reproduce this book or portions thereof in any form whatsoever. No part of this book may be used or reproduced by any means, graphic, electronic, or mechanical, including photocopying, recording, taping or by any information storage retrieval system without the written permission of the author except in the case of brief quotations embodied in critical articles and reviews.]

CONTENTS

An Introduction to the Book	7
About Author	9
The Waste Land as a Modernist Text of Poetry	10
Abstract	11
An Introduction to Modernism in 20th Century Literature	12
The Waste Land as a Modernist Text of Poetry	19
Conclusion	22
References	23
Unity of Being as a Philosophy in Yeats`s Poetry	24
Abstract	25
'Unity of Being' as a Philosophy in Yeats`s Poetry	26
Conclusion	28
References	29
Read More	30

AN INTRODUCTION TO THE BOOK

'odernism In TS Eliot's The Waste Land: Decoding Elements of Modernism in Literature' is a short and critical essay on *T. S. Eliot's 'The Waste Land'* as a text of modernist poetry. The book examines the prominent and easily discernible elements in the poem The Waste Land that make it a profoundly modernist text of poetry. For students to acquaint themselves with the literary subject of modernism in literature, the author has devoted a separate chapter to the topic under the heading of,

Shafqat Mushtaq

An Introduction to Modernism in 20th Century Literature.

In addition, the book also contains a supplementary essay on *W. B. Yeats`s poetry* entitled **'Unity of Being as a Philosophy in Yeats`s Poetry'**. It will be especially helpful in understanding his poem *Among School Children*.

In short, whether you are studying Eliot as an undergraduate or graduate student, this book is must-read in the sense that it deals with modernism in Eliot`s poetry in a detailed and well-researched manner.

For complete appreciation of The Waste Land, undertaking the study of literary modernism is extremely important. It will be helpful in dealing with the poetry of T. S. Eliot in particular, other modern poets in general.

Shafqat Mushtaq

ABOUT AUTHOR

Shafqat Mushtaq holds masters in English Literature from the University of Kashmir. He is the author of **Blossoms from Elsewhere, Defy Odds and Be Unstoppable, JM Coetzee`s Disgrace and Racism in Post-Apartheid South Africa, 1984 George Orwell (Book Analysis): Reading the Novel in Post-Trump Context by Shafqat Mushtaq,** and is published frequently in leading English dailies of Kashmir.

Shafqat Mushtaq

THE WASTE LAND AS A MODERNIST TEXT OF POETRY

ABSTRACT

The objective of this essay is to examine the prominent and discernible elements that make T.S. Eliot's poem *The Waste Land* a profoundly modernist text of poetry. Out of many features that permeate every single line of *The Waste Land*, the focus of this assignment centers on the concept of the *Subjectivity and Objectivity*, and *Fragmentation* (literary, social and individual).

AN INTRODUCTION TO MODERNISM IN 20TH CENTURY LITERATURE

The thing or idea that stands out prominently in *The Waste Land* of T.S. Eliot is its sharp drift from the individual consciousness – not a complete abandonment of it – towards a more inclusive and collective exploration of a myriad of consciences typical of the times of Eliot. To delve deep into the meaning of such a drift, as undertaken by T.S. Eliot, demands a deeper exploration of the topic.

Edmund Wilson writes an essay by the title *"The

Rag-Bag of the Soul" and includes such works as Eliot`s *The Waste Land*, Joyce`s *Ulysses* and works of other such writers as Ezra Pound, Virginia Wolf and Sherwood Anderson under the umbrella of texts he considers show the modernist tendency. For him, they are the torch-bearers of modernism in the 20th century English Literature. The foundation of his classification rests on the claim that these writers focus, or speak from the point of view of the human consciousness of an individual and the way they show the reader how "the whole world [is] sunk in the subjective life of a single human soul – beyond whose vague and impassable walls there is nothing solid and clear".

What he means is that beyond the individual subjectivity, or the individual consciousness of an individual, there exists nothing objective, or to which one can assign the objectivity. Fair enough to say that what`s outside is murky waters and nothing else.

Another distinctive feature of modernism dominant in the literature of these writers, according to Edmund Wilson, is the fragmentation. The sort of fragmentation that Wilson points out and reflects on includes not only the literary fragmentation – the way Eliot has suffused *The Waste Land* with quotations from past writers and the literature they have produced shows that it exists only in the broken forms, in patches without a fuller picture, and it also shows that people have not been able to completely abandon, or wipe out, the literary marvel of past masters but have it imprinted somewhere on their minds.

The literary man of modern times may not know the complete wisdom of Shakespeare or Chaucer or Buddha, yet their wisdom still exists in bits and pieces and that is shown brilliantly by Eliot the way he goes on quoting Shakespeare here and Chaucer there – but individual and social as well.

Fragmentation means, out of many things, an absence of common worldview; lack of something solid and well-defined towards which one can turn to, or show allegiance to. What then according to Edmund Wilson represents modernity in literary texts is an individual soul cocooned in subjectivity, but at the same time fragmented within it (individual soul). It is due to the inability of the individual to "pick up the scattered pieces" that such a fragmentation exists.

"Heap of broken images" from *The Waste Land* bears the testimony to the same concept of fragmentation Edmund Wilson talks about. In fact, there could be no better elucidation, or a graphic representation, of the state of isolated fragmentation than Eliot`s vivid and profound line, "heap of broken images".

But there is an irony associated with Wilson`s claim of *subjectivity* in Eliot`s poetry, or for that matter in the poetry of Ezra Pound as well.

According to Wilson subjectivity dominates, what

he calls, the "newer poetry" and cites the works of Eliot and Pound to substantiate his finding. But when Eliot and Pound are studied independently, there is enough substance in their works to prove that they both were stern critiques of subjectivity.

It was prominent in the poetry of their predecessors and they detested it by saying that subjectivity "distorts reality and fails to render experience faithfully". It was in the same interest that Pound launched the Imagist project in 1910 to bring *objectivity* to individual consciousness and subjectivity so that what an individual mind perceives can be rendered comprehensible to a larger audience, or to bring it on the platform of collective experience.

Eliot, too, advocates the same ideology as is evident in his poem *The Waste Land* where no single voice drives the narrative. He leaps one step further and goes beyond individual consciousness. He makes objectivity his tool to reveal underlying truths caught in the net of the subjectivity of individual human consciousness through external objects and sources from other literary texts.

The fragmentation which is one of the prominent features of *The Waste Land* further illustrates why he would vouch for scattered voices when individual consciousness was a norm. He does not abandon subjectivity though but brings objectivity to its shores for proper exploration of the reality. In simple terms, it can be said about Eliot that he derives, or inheres subjectivity from the Tradition (as is evident in *Tradition and the Individual Talent*) but drives on objectivity.

The philosophical and critical discourse on the literature of later half of 19th and early 20th century confined itself mostly to the philosophy of consciousness and subjectivity. Riding on the same wave the novelists of this period embraced these concepts and the influence began to show up in their writings, especially in the manner the narrative remained confined to a single narrator and his consciousness and perspectives. Techniques like *Stream of Consciousness* bear the same imprint.

Henry Bergson wrote extensively on the question of consciousness and thought it as the primary source of our knowledge of reality. He calls "the raw subjective flux of sensations and impressions" fundamental to our understanding of the world of reality. His philosophy deeply influenced T.E. Hulme, T.S. Eliot, Ezra Pound and others to the point that an imagist movement was launched to make literature of the time a faithful representation and tool for the communication of "sense impressions".

In addition to that what these poets sought to do was bringing objectivity to the already subjective subject matter; it was an attempt to replace emotions with facts; individual fancy, or experience, or perception with collective and larger reality.

That possibly could be the reason behind Eliot`s

praise of James Joyce when he complimented him by saying that James was "the most intelligent man of his generation" and that his novels were commendable for "for maintaining a point of view". So, it is fair enough to say that the point of view or subjectivity has remained at the forefront of modernism.

It helped the modern poets to do away with the obsession their predecessors had with "big things" and "epic subjects"; instead they aimed to imbibe the subjective perception emanating from the real and factual world and received by human consciousness through sensations and impressions.

Hulme`s words further elaborate how modern poetry is different from that of the old when he says, "[modern poetry] has become definitely and finally introspective and deals with the expression and communication of momentary phases in the poet`s mind". It lays bare before us the tendencies of the modernism, which included consciousness and subjectivity tinged with the streaks of objectivity.

Though Eliot believed in the same assumptions as Hulme and Pound, or as propounded by Bergson, yet at the same time he also tried to expose the limitations of subjectivity and made substantial attempts to go beyond the individual consciousness. Catastrophic events like World War First and its harsh repercussions – in the form of massive inflations, civil wars, lack of central and unified ideology, and the outbreak of anarchy – these events compelled Eliot and other poets to not neglect the 'public' when exploring an 'individual'.

He did not, however, completely forget the principles, styles, and the philosophy handed down to him by the 'tradition' in his pursuit of complete adherence to the modernism. He would not have thought, otherwise, of writing a long epic poem had it not been for the tradition. It is like weaving the same thread into a different cloth.

Therefore, in Eliot, it is absolutely legitimate to sense a sort intermix of traditional and modern impulses, along with the influence of philosophy of the time, and same is the reason why *The Waste Land* is utterly unique in its content, style, and language.

THE WASTE LAND AS A MODERNIST TEXT OF POETRY

Now that background information on processes, philosophical and literary, going on during the early 20th century that produced modernism has already been deliberated on, what remains next is text, *The Waste Land*, itself. *The Waste Land* was written during the time of annihilation of the old world; replaced by a new one with no center in sight – which Yeats beautifully puts as *"Turning and turning in the widening gyre ... Things fall apart; the centre cannot hold"*.

The political circumstances of the time witnessed a rampant upheaval, especially after the end of First World War. Be that inflation in Germany, civil war in Ireland, the violent revolution in Russia, and it was also the time when women were given the right to vote, education was universalized, yet a sense of unreality was there pertaining to the way the world was still jammed together not blown apart completely even after undergoing World War One and Two. It is there but it is no longer the same world anymore. It is full of chaos and destruction. It is dead like a waste land from which nothing good can sprout – *"… what branches grow out of this stony rubbish?"*

Another important thing that happened was the creation of BBC and introduction of radio plays. All these conditions triggered poets to respond differently to the reality that was let loose on the world. It needed apart from subjective, an objective treatment to look beyond the façade – *"Son of man, You cannot say, or guess, for you only know A heap of broken images …"*

They have a bearing on the poetry of T.S. Eliot and *The Waste Land* is the finest example. The critics are of the opinion that it reads more like a radio play than a traditional epic, and we know with the advent of BBC radio plays became immensely popular during the time of T.S. Eliot.

Loss of unity, doubt and uncertainty was as much in the outside world – though modern man himself may not have been aware of such obscurity or pretended to believe otherwise by looking at the positive side of modernity such as technological advancement, that makes it clear how objectivity can help poets to reveal underlying and subtle truths and reality – as it is in the text of *The Waste Land* – *"Unreal city, Under the brown fog of a winter dawn,*

A crowd flowed over London Bridge, so many, I had not thought death had undone so many ...".

The form and structure of *The Waste Land* follow no specific order. Modern poets sought to break away with the use of meter and formal structure, that way also *The Waste Land* is a modernist text of poetry as it is written in free verse and follows no specific rhyme scheme.

It explores thoroughly the individual consciousness as exhibited by various characters in the poem and brings objectivity to the subjective stance of these characters by using real objects, real locations, and references to real texts. Doing so universalizes the message, makes truth conveyable to a larger audience because they can relate to it objectively.

The literary fragmentation of the time finds its way in the poem as well. In one instance Eliot goes on to quote Shakespeare and next moment it is the popular song, one minute it is Chaucer and next quotes from Bible and Buddha. It is fractured into multiple voices.

CONCLUSION

The Waste Land is the modernist text of poetry, exhibiting modernism both in *form and structure* and the *subject matter*. The way it has been composed, its incoherence in narrative technique, broken imagery, bringing subjectivity and objectivity together, its despair and decentralization of meaning all go on to prove that The Waste Land indeed has captured profoundly the mood and the circumstance of the modern life, a life so severely crippled to walk upright.

REFERENCES

1: Alvaro Marin, University of New Castle, *English Modernist Poetry – T.S. Eliot`s The Waste Land.* (Published on Research Gate)

2: Mohammad Jamal Al-Amleh, Al-Quds University, *T.S. Eliot`s Poem: The Waste Land in the Eyes of Modernism.*

3: Prof. Radhika Subhankar Mukherjee, Dnyanasadhana College, Thane, *A Study of Ecology as a Metaphor in T.S. Eliot`s The Waste Land.* (Published on Research Scholar)

4: Wassim Rustom, University of Oslo, *Poetics and The Waste Land – Subjects, Objects and the "Poem Including History."*

5: Text of *The Waste Land* by T.S. Eliot.

Shafqat Mushtaq

UNITY OF BEING AS A PHILOSOPHY IN YEATS`S POETRY

ABSTRACT

The essay attempts to explore W.B. Yeats`s implementation of *unity of being* philosophy in the poetry he wrote, especially in the poem *"Among School Children"*.

'UNITY OF BEING' AS A PHILOSOPHY IN YEATS`S POETRY

Yeats has set a standard for himself. He wants to unify. He wants to join dots. When he says *"Hammer your thoughts into unity"* the critics of his work sort of tend to explore Yeats in the same light. They take out various aspects of his life and attempt to knit them together into a unified meaningful whole.

His unity lies in the resolution of the conflict between two opposites, "the material and the spiritual" and he successfully achieves that in his poetry. In the poem *"Among School Children"* a visit to the school confronts the speaker of the poem, or W.B.

Yeats himself, with present, past and the future at the same time.

On seeing the children, his thoughts shift towards Maud Gonne, which means to the memory of her from the distant past. "I dream of a Ledaean body, bent above a sinking fire, a tale that she ..."

At the same time, he experiences a sort of transformation he and Maud Gonne have gone through from he being not a "Leaden kind" and she with "that color upon her cheek or hair" that had his heart "driven wild", from that youthful stage to that him being now a "kind of old scarecrow" and she "hollow of cheek as though it drank the wind".

His thoughts don`t stop here as he goes on to visualize the future of "a shape upon her lap", or the child. He achieves the unity among these various stages as a result of his smooth switching between them and they exist before him in a unified manner. He unifies the memory and the man and sees them together as a whole.

He mentions Plato – "to alter Plato`s parable, Into the yolk and white of the one shell" – for specific reasons and that is to achieve or substantiate the philosophy of *Unity of Being*. Plato had the opinion that "human being was one" and that they separated into two only to be unified later in the time. In the sphere not only there is the physical unity but spiritual as well.

CONCLUSION

Towards the end of the poem, Yeats achieves the unity by resolving the opposites. He finds the unity between body and soul, physical and spiritual by says that a dancer cannot be separated from the dance. In his poetry Yeats does not simply go on implementing the unity, he firstly separates various entities and put them opposite to one another – for example, the youth and old. Then he resolves the conflict between them and says that they actually exist in one another like a dancer in the dance. So what we understand from "Among School Children" is the implementation of the "Unity of Being" philosophy that he always regarded highly.

REFERENCES

1: Text of *Among School Children* by W. B. Yeats.

2: Shin, Wonkyung, Hanyang University, *"Among School Children": Search for Unity of Being*. (Published in The Yeats Journal of Korea)

3: K. N. Sharma, *"Among School Children by William Butler Yeats: Critical Appreciation"*.

READ MORE

1984 George Orwell (Book Analysis): Reading the Novel in Post-Trump Context by Shafqat Mushtaq

J.M. Coetzee`s Disgrace and Racism in Post-Apartheid South Africa: A Postcolonial Analysis by Shafqat Mushtaq

Blossoms From Elsewhere by Shafqat Mushtaq

Defy Odds and Be Unstoppable: Real Life Inspirational Stories – Transforming Dreams into Actions by Shafqat Mushtaq

Printed in Great Britain
by Amazon